Managing

People

YOUR SELF-DEVELOPMENT ACTION PLAN

PETER GRAINGER

NP

Kogan Page Ltd, London
Nichols Publishing Company,
New Jersey

First published in 1994

Apart from any fair dealing for the purposes of research or
private study, or criticism, as permitted under the Copyright,
Designs and Patents Act, 1988, this publication may only be
reproduced, stored or transmitted, in any form or by any means,
with the prior permission in writing of the publishers, or in the
case of reprographic reproduction in accordance with the terms of
licences issued by the Copyright Licensing Agency. Enquiries
concerning reproduction outside those terms should be sent to the
publishers at the undermentioned address:

Kogan Page Limited
120 Pentonville Road
London N1 9JN

© Peter Grainger, 1994

Published in the United States of America by Nichols Publishing,
PO Box 6036, East Brunswick, New Jersey 08816

British Library Cataloguing in Publication Data

A CIP record for this book is available from the British Library.

ISBN (UK) 0 7494 1249 6
ISBN (US) 0-89397-434-X

Typeset by the author
Printed and bound in Great Britain by Biddles Ltd, Guildford and
King's Lynn.

CONTENTS

4   Contents

PREFACE

It has taken more than 20 years to refine the 12 generic skills of management, which are the foundation of the Manager's Toolkit series, into a form which is both straightforward enough for busy managers to learn and which actually works in real life.

The skills contained in the original *Manager's Toolkit* manual and the linked style definitions were developed in the course of 15 years' management experience in senior training and development positions with Rank Xerox. Unique opportunities existed in the company at that time for creative approaches to the training and development of first-level and middle managers on both sides of the Atlantic.

As a member of a number of specialist teams in the USA and Europe, I was fortunate to come into personal contact with many of the most effective management techniques of recent times – for example, the systematic approach of Charles Kepner and Ben Tregoe and the Huthwaite Research Group's 'Interactive Skills'.

The first step was to build these techniques into a set of 'Management Standards' which the management teams of Rank Xerox's manufacturing plants in the UK developed over a number of years, and then test them in *practical* situations, including residential training programmes.

Every manager participating in a training programme brought a real-life problem to the course, and the skills taught were applied to each of those 'issues' during the programme. If a technique did not work or took too long to apply, it was discarded or modified.

After ten years of running intensive management development programmes at all levels, we had so refined the techniques that they could be integrated into a comprehensive 'toolkit' of skills that would actually guarantee results (pages 10–12).

At this time, my later business partner, Roger Acland, and I developed the personal style definitions which became an essential ingredient of all our work, and from which I later created the 'Personal Development Toolkit' and the Style Profile (page 37).

This integrated learning approach, built upon the need for positive thinking (page 26), has proved its special value to groups of managers and potential managers drawn from a wide range of organizations, from students, accountants, and engineers to teams in Allied Lyons, Rank Xerox and British Telecom.

The great benefit of the approach is that it is quick to use, flexible – *and it works*. After years of practical application, the 12 skills have now been honed to such simple effectiveness that they can be readily acquired through open learning. Look through the structure and methodology of the book to see how the approach works in practice for the three 'People' skills contained in this manual.

I believe the hundreds of organizations of all sizes that have purchased the original *Manager's Toolkit* manual since its publication in 1992 provide ample confirmation of the simple effectiveness of both the content and the method of learning.

Peter Grainger

INTRODUCTION

INTRODUCTION

1. The approach

The Manager's Toolkit series is designed to be suitable for a wide range of managers. You may already be a manager responsible for the work of other people and want to learn how to make more of yourself and the resources under your control. You may be facing the prospect of the responsibility of managing – or you may want to take an opportunity to manage when it arises – and be uncertain how to set about it.

To make the most of the books in the series you will either not have received any management training or the training you have received will have only given you *knowledge* of management and not the practical skills of *how* to manage.

Statistics show that few managers have received any formal training. I suspect most managers are too busy – or too exhausted – to find time to study 'management' literature. The style of each book in the series is therefore as economical and as visual as possible, concentrating on making clear each step of each process or skill – more like a DIY car manual than a learned business treatise.

The series will not only explain the essential generic skills of managing yourself and others but will give you opportunities to *practise* those skills as you apply them to your own real-life situations. The comprehensive Index on pages 95 and 96 provides you with easy access when you have a specific skills need.

In addition to acquiring such essential skills as specifying targets and standards and chairing meetings, you will come to understand yourself better, the person behind the manager or potential manager.

Some people master some of the skills of management more readily than others because of the sort of *person* they are. Some people are good with information but not with people, others are good with people but poor at taking action.

You will analyse your *personal style* in relation to three style definitions and as a result determine which are the most important skills for you personally to work on (see pages 38-9). You can therefore create your own development plan from the moment you buy the first book, confident that you are using your learning time most effectively.

Finally, you will gradually build up a *positive approach* to the situations in which you find yourself as a manager. Developing positive expectations of people and situations is a critical part of leadership and management. It has to be acquired and continuously worked at. It is not just a matter of attitude, but of applying particular techniques. Anyone can learn these techniques and so make a remarkable difference not only to the way they manage but also to the impact they make on the world about them.

2. The toolkit of skills

The Manager's Toolkit series consists of four personal development workbooks designed as open learning training and development aids to enable anyone who wants to be able to manage – or manage better – to acquire the necessary skills in their own time and at their own pace.

The series is based on the single volume *The Manager's Toolkit*, which I published in 1992, and was bought by large numbers of human resource specialists in large and small organizations throughout the United Kingdom. It was felt that making the *Toolkit* available *as a series* in a smaller format at lower cost would bring it within reach of individual managers and potential managers as and when they required each group of skills.

The concept of an *integrated* 'toolkit' of skills provides you with the opportunity to use the skills in sequence (for example in a major project), or skill-by-skill according to your personal need.

The formation of the toolkit shown opposite was the basis of the original *Manager's Toolkit*. The 12 key skills emerged from more complex models, and in numerical sequence represent a sequential, cyclical *process of management*, from clarifying roles (1) to giving and receiving feedback (12).

Each skill is not only important in its own right, but also links with its neighbour in making up *clusters* of skills for particular purposes, for example in this model to provide a

The Toolkit of Skills

a process of management

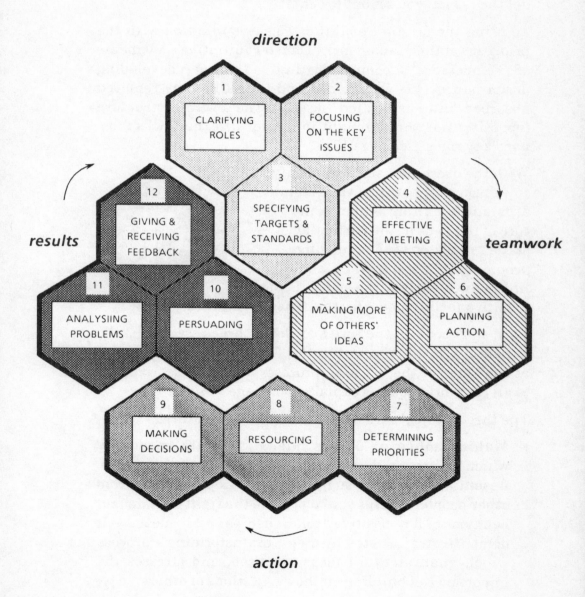

direction

1 CLARIFYING ROLES

2 FOCUSING ON THE KEY ISSUES

3 SPECIFYING TARGETS & STANDARDS

4 EFFECTIVE MEETING

12 GIVING & RECEIVING FEEDBACK

results

teamwork

11 ANALYSIING PROBLEMS

10 PERSUADING

5 MAKING MORE OF OTHERS' IDEAS

6 PLANNING ACTION

9 MAKING DECISIONS

8 RESOURCING

7 DETERMINING PRIORITIES

action

© PETER GRAINGER 1994

sense of *direction*, to help your group to work as a *team*, to get plans turned into *action* or to make sure you actually get the *results* you set out to achieve.

To bring the original toolkit of 12 skills into line with the priorities of the Management Charter Initiative's 'elements of competence', 'communicating' (7) and 'developing performance' (11) were added and the skills they replaced absorbed into associated skills. The overall structure (opposite) was then brought into line with the MCI's four-part 'key roles' (see page 17).

With the *operations* skills of 'clarifying roles', 'specifying targets and standards' and 'planning action' at the core of the toolkit, the particular skills associated with managing *people*, *resources* and *information* link conveniently with each of them to form a toolkit model for the series.

Each workbook in the series explores three essential skills in depth, providing opportunities for *open learning* practice at each step of the learning process. The process, common to all the workbooks, is explained on pages 18–19.

The three 'people' skills covered by this volume are:

- **Making more of others' ideas** (5) is the means by which you make the most of the creativity of your team. Assuming you want suggestions for improvement from other people, it helps you to provide the right climate and behaviour for positive relationships and ideas. It demonstrates a step-by-step 'brainstorming' process which guarantees all ideas are used, and stresses the importance of building on the suggestions of others.

The Manager's Toolkit Series

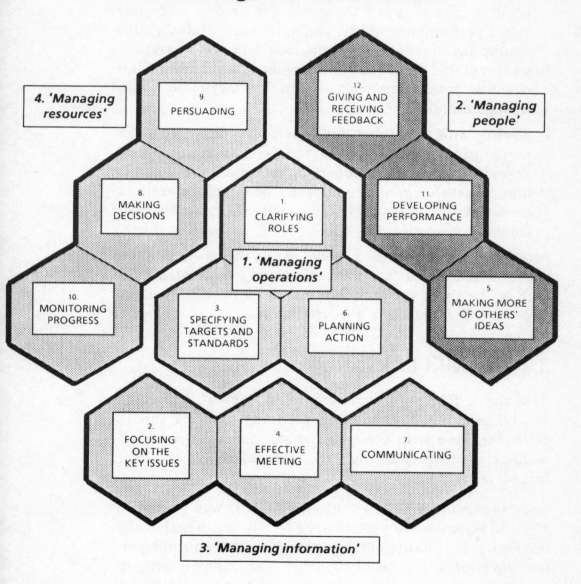

- **Developing performance** (11) covers the steps that you need to take to make the most of your own and your staff's performance, short- and long-term. It deals with appropriate managerial behaviour and the analytical tools required for effective development preparation, and suggests specific methods of actually developing those with potential.

- **Giving and receiving feedback** (12) deals with the preparation and behaviour required to counsel and appraise individual members of your staff. It suggests how to develop joint action plans for improvement and development, and how to benefit from individual feedback yourself.

After each skills chapter a model shows the skills in other books in the series that are most closely associated with each of the three skills in this workbook, so that you can develop your expertise in a focused manner.

3. The MCI links

Creating a four-part series from the original *Manager's Toolkit* manual provided an opportunity to bring the 12 skills into line with the national standards for first line managers developed by the Management Charter Initiative.

The Management Charter Initiative (MCI) was formed in 1988 'to improve the performance of UK organisations by improving the quality of UK managers'. It is an employer-led, government-backed body calling for improvements in the quality, quantity, relevance and accessibility of management education and development.

After extensive consultation, research and testing, the MCI is establishing a framework of four levels for management and supervisory development (Supervisory, Certificate, Diploma and Masters), with assessments based on demonstrated ability to manage. The guidelines at each of these levels give clear guidance on what is expected of managers at different levels, providing specific requirements for their development and assessment.

Detailed standards have been established for Supervisors, First Level Managers and Middle Managers, and I have taken the *First Level Management Standards* as the most appropriate link to the skills in the Manager's Toolkit series. They provide the management reference point for the National Vocational Qualifications at Level 4.

The standards first break down the key *roles* of management into *units* and *elements of competence*. Those covered in this workbook are:

Manage People

5 Develop teams, individuals and self to enhance performance
5.1 Develop and improve teams through planning and activities
5.2 Identify, review and improve development activities for individuals
5.3 Develop oneself within the job role

6 Plan allocate and **evaluate work carried out by teams, individuals and self**
6.3 (Allocate work) and evaluate teams, individuals and self against objectives
6.4 Provide feedback to teams and individuals on their performance

7 Create, maintain and enhance effective working relationships
7.1–2 Establish and maintain the trust and support of one's subordinates and of one's immediate manager
7.3 Establish and maintain relationships with colleagues
7.4 Identify and minimize interpersonal conflict
(7.5 Implement disciplinary and grievance procedures)
7.6 Counsel staff

Managing Resources has been broadened beyond 'manage finance' to cover *all resources* and includes 'making decisions', a skill which is essential to 'contribute to the recruitment and selection of personnel' (*Unit 4, opposite*).

The first three elements of Unit 6 – '*plan, allocate...work*' – have been included in the 'operations' workbook because they link effectively with clarifying roles, tasks and plans.

As a result, a number of references in Element 6.4 (eg 'organizational guidelines' and 'systems/procedures') link directly with the skills in that workbook, rather than the skills in this.

Unit 5 and the remainder of Units 6 and 7 (see opposite) focus on *developing and evaluating* teams, individuals and self, and on creating effective *working relationships*.

You will therefore find the emphasis in this workbook will be on the review and development of *individual* performance, and on positive relationships within the *team*, built on open behaviour and sharing ideas. (There will be no specific references to Element 7.5, 'Implement disciplinary and grievance procedures').

Some of the open learning activities relating to development (eg pages 62–6) are equally beneficial to you, to individual members of your staff or to complete teams. Giving and *receiving* feedback encourages the open behaviour between individual and manager, advocated by the MCI in Element 7.2.

MCI key roles and units of competence for first line managers

Manage Operations

1 Maintain and improve service and product operations

2 Contribute to the implementation of change in services, products and systems

Manage Finance

3 Recommend, monitor and control the use of resources

Manage Resources

4 Contribute to the recruitment and selection of personnel

Manage People

5 *Develop teams, individuals and self to enhance performance*

6 (Plan, allocate and) *evaluate work carried out by teams, individuals and self*

7 *Create, maintain and enhance effective working relationships*

Manage Information

8 Seek, evaluate and organize information for action

9 Exchange information to solve problems and make decisions

Individual and group involvement, represented by phrases such as 'offers of ideas' and 'proposals for action', are supported with specific techniques in the chapters on ideas and feedback. And you will find the means of achieving 'honest and constructive relationships' and 'open, honest and friendly behaviour' (Unit 7) throughout all three skills chapters.

4. The method of learning

The book is laid out with explanations of each skill on the left and blank forms on the right for you to complete step-by-step in parallel with each explanation. You will find it helpful to read through *the whole* of the explanation for each chapter on the left before starting to complete the practice forms on the right, in order to see each step in its context.

In the practice forms on the right you will always be asked for information from *your own work situation*, so that the effort you put in will be repaid by consistently providing you with practical material for use on the job. At the bottom of each box on every practice sheet you will find sample answers to guide you towards your own answer.

The explanation and practice sheets for each of the three skills are followed first by a completed worksheet or questionnaire, and then by an identical blank format for you to fill in for yourself.

The *worksheet* is designed to pull together all the steps of each process and to act as a summary of the skill you have just worked through; it is also a useful reminder of the skill as you look for opportunities to practise. The *questionnaires* act as checklists for each skill *after* practising, and should be completed as soon as possible after the experience.

The process works like this:

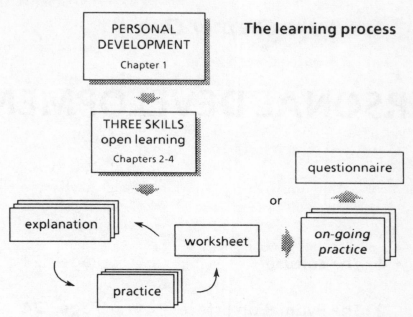

The learning process

After the open learning practice available in this book, first section-by-section, step-by-step, and then on each summary worksheet, *immediate practice* at work to secure the skills is most important. But valuable practice opportunities also exist *outside* the working environment in low risk domestic or social situations.

You may be frustrated by a committee you attend because nobody seems to listen to anyone else's ideas. Or perhaps you know a young person who has no idea of a career and wants some help. Have you ever had a disagreement with a neighbour or friend and not known how to resolve it face-to-face? The relevant skills can be found in this workbook!

You do not learn to drive a car or to play the piano, for example, without *regular practice* – learning the skills of management has just the same requirement.

Chapter One

PERSONAL DEVELOPMENT

PERSONAL DEVELOPMENT

1. The culture

The management climate and cultural standards that direct behaviour at work have a profound influence on effective personal development. The role model we provide for our staff or the way our own manager behaves towards us creates an environment that can make or break our willingness and ability to develop ourselves.

In terms of managing people, I believe, management has for too long suffered from the illusion that its effective operation depends on use of 'head' and not 'heart'. When managers are prepared to show that they have feelings and that they *care* – about people as well as about the success of the enterprise – the response from their staff is immediate and surprising. We follow leaders who are human as well as decisive, and who seem to have a warmth of personality to which we can readily respond.

This ability to care and respond – the MCI's 'open, honest and friendly behaviour' – not only creates a more positive and pleasant environment in which to work, but is also highly productive. Teams in which people are open with each other, and in which the group members care about the effectiveness, development and well-being of others, soon become highly productive and creative units.

But how about the MCI's 'honesty'? I genuinely believe that *integrity* is an essential ingredient for effective people management, but one which seems to have become discredited of late. Treating people fairly and consistently actually makes good long-term business sense. A manager may get away with 'short-changing' staff once or twice, but long-term, as individuals' trust seeps away, they will either try to get back at the manager concerned, or will only work to the minimum standards required to keep their jobs.

If you want creativity from your people, and 'breakthrough' ideas which can make your business uniquely competitive, your people need to be relaxed and trusting in their relationships, and sufficiently motivated to produce that extra dimension of performance that comes from enthusiastic commitment to the leader. It's old-fashioned 'carrot, rather than stick' motivation, I suppose!

To achieve this level of commitment, you need to know your people *as people*, and be in sufficiently regular touch with them as individuals that you are promptly aware when something is not going right. Reviewing performance on a *one-to-one and regular basis* is critical to managing people. So often managers believe that group reviews at meetings are quite sufficient – they are not!

Making time for people – being willing to consider their ideas, informally listening to their problems, discussing their targets, talking over their development needs – is desperately difficult to do in the pressurized situation in which managers find themselves today. But this disciplined investment in time will soon produce a dramatic return in terms of commitment and results.

After all, the manager's role is to *get things done through other people*, not to be doing them him- or herself. We are all aware of the importance of delegation, and yet managers these days are expected to be seen rushing around, working late, and stressed. Being under pressure, or putting your staff under constant pressure, may be a macho status symbol for some managers, but it is no way to get the best from your people.

Personal development, and the practice of the skills recently learnt, requires patience and time – time to take risks and to fail. Managers, as effective coaches, need the courage to allow those working for them the time and opportunity to build confidence, to develop, to share ideas, in order to realize their full potential.

Personal development requires a longer-term perspective than we have been used to of late, and one which is critical to the effective deployment of *any* resource in any enterprise, let alone the one which we hear *ad nauseam* is 'our most important asset'!

The self-teach open learning method of this workbook will help you to take increasing responsibility for developing *your own* 'people' skills as and when you need them, in your own time and at your own pace. Your performance should then continuously improve and develop in a culture in which your management openly encourages and supports your efforts, and provides the feedback and opportunities for practice.

2.   The Pygmalion Effect

The way management is performed around us creates a culture in which we feel able – or not – to develop our full potential. Similarly the right *attitude* is critical to managing ourselves and other people, and the development of a *positive* attitude is required before setting out to acquire particular skills. Understanding the Pygmalion Effect is a major step in the right direction.

The essence of the Pygmalion Effect lies in the power of positive *expectations*. The word 'Pygmalion' comes not from George Bernard Shaw but from Greek mythology. Pygmalion was a sculptor in Cyprus who carved a statue of a girl which was so beautiful that he fell in love with it. So powerful were his expectations and his will that Venus stepped in and turned the statue into human form – and they both lived happily ever after!

Positive thinking has been proved to be critical to success; positive expectations of an outcome increase the likelihood of a successful result. The conscious development of positive thinking and of high expectations of ourselves and others can have a remarkable effect on our confidence, our relationships and our success.

And yet the most natural response to unknown people and uncertain situations is *negative*. So often, both individually and in groups, we display negative rather than positive responses. Often it is because we are uncertain. Uncertainty leads to fear and fear to expectations of failure – a self-fulfilling prophecy.

2. The Pygmalion Effect

2.1 Write down a difficult situation with which you have recently had to deal:

I had to reprimand a difficult member of my staff

2.2 What was your attitude to this situation when you approached it, or your expectations of the person when you came into contact?

I expected him not to accept it and to blame David

What was the effect of your attitude on what happened?

Opening very tense; I was looking for the reaction

2.3 If your approach was negative, how might you have been more positive towards the situation or the person concerned?

Maybe he wasn't happy with his performance either. Move quickly to joint plan for improvement

To manage effectively we have consciously and continuously to fill the vacuum of uncertainty with positive expectations. We need to make a specific and conscious effort to identify the positive elements in any situation and the strengths of any individual. 'Is the glass half-full or half-empty?' *It is remarkable how easy it is to think of the positive factors in a situation if we just stop and consider for a moment.*

Once we have tried to be positive about situations and people, we can even try a little *enthusiasm*! Enthusiasm is an essential ingredient in getting things done successfully, particularly when we want help from other people. They may be suspicious at first, but they will find it difficult not to respond.

But positive thinking, and particularly enthusiasm, need to be *demonstrated* for the Pygmalion Effect to work. The influence we have on other people results directly from the way we behave towards them. If we are in the habit of treating people in a way that conveys trust and high expectations, a positive response, and so positive results, are likely to follow. A smile at the right moment can have a dramatic effect.

Confidence of course affects whether we manage situations positively or negatively. We require confidence in ourselves in order to have a positive effect on other people, and to have that confidence we need to *understand ourselves*, to be aware of our natural strengths and to recognize our limitations. The next section will enable you to do just that.

2.4 Write down a situation in the future that you are uncertain about, a situation where you don't know what is likely to happen:	*I've got to tell Jim that his ideas on policy revisions have not been accepted*
2.5 What are your expectations of that situation? If your expectations are negative, how is it likely to affect the outcome?	*He'll take it personally - 'No-one's interested in my ideas'* *I'll be looking for the reaction and be ready with my arguments - he may not even be upset*
2.6 Think of the positive factors involved and how you could use them to make your expectations more positive.	*Reasons for rejection do make sense. Boss had asked for his ideas*

3. Personal style

Our ability to manage some situations and not others, to manage some people and not others, is partly a question of the sort of person we are, our personal style. If we understood more about our style it would help us to know and to develop our natural strengths and to accept or overcome our limitations.

The three styles we developed are very simple and represent the basis of 'what makes people tick'.   They first emerged as a result of considering an interesting model of motivation, which exactly reflected the result of the research we were doing at the time into leadership styles and the means of identifying *potential* managers.

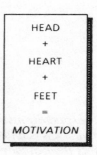

HEAD
+
HEART
+
FEET
=
MOTIVATION

The first distinct style is **'Analyse'** (or 'Head') to represent the thinking, analytical type of person; the second is **'Bond'** (or 'Heart'), the feeling, caring type of person; the third is **'Command'** (or 'Feet'), the active, results-orientated type of person.

Each style can be summed up as follows:

'ANALYSE' (or 'Head')

Values logic and distrusts subjective judgements; able to provide considered and rational arguments; keen to see rules and procedures applied.

'BOND' (or 'Heart')

Conscious of the importance of mutual understanding and stresses the benefits of working with people; seeks to get the best out of others by trust and encouragement.

'COMMAND' (or 'Feet')

Likes to be in control of people and events, quickly responding to job demands and opportunities; trusts own judgement and acts on conclusions; inclined to use incentives and sanctions to influence results.

A high-scoring 'Analyse' type of person is likely to be quiet and methodical, a conscientious administrator who likes to get things right. A predominantly 'Bond' person is likely to be open with emotions and conscious of the importance of other people, a visible carer with individuals or inside a team. A 'Command' person is likely to be impatient for results and to know instinctively what needs doing, an entrepreneur or 'born organizer'.

But people rarely fit a style description exactly. People are usually a mixture of the three styles, generally of just two of them. *Few of us have the capacity to spread equally across all three.* We often have one which is an area of weakness which tends to ruin our all round performance, but which provides a focus for our personal development.

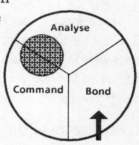

There are of course many current methods of identifying personal style. Generally, though, they provide you with an interesting profile but no plan of action to aid your development, and almost certainly no links to learnable management skills.

However, one of the benefits of the 'toolkit' approach is that the skills within the toolkit can be re-assembled into different shapes for different purposes. The skills in the Personal Development Toolkit overleaf have been re-assembled to match the most appropriate style.

'Analyse' covers the *information*-providing skills ('monitoring', 'clarifying', 'specifying' and 'focusing'), skills associated with individual thinking processes.

'Bond' covers skills associated with being with *people* ('making more of others' ideas', 'giving and receiving feedback', 'communicating' and 'meeting'), skills most effective when done with openness and feeling.

The 'Command' skills are all related to taking *action* and getting results ('persuading', 'planning action', 'making decisions' and 'developing performance').

In the style questionnaire overleaf you are asked to consider yourself in relation to 12 straightforward statements. How far does each statement represent a fair description of you? Circle the appropriate number against each statement, and then circle the number in the next column to indicate the extent to which you would like to change the rating you have given yourself.

At the centre of the personal development model opposite are the core skills of 'specifying targets and standards', 'making more of others' ideas' and 'planning action' (in italics). These are the essence of the integrated style – **'Drive'** – which contains elements of the other three styles. It is the basis of a balanced *leadership* – and of an effective management – style:

Clear and positive in thinking towards future possibilities; capable of generating enthusiasm and a flexible approach to achieving results; is sensitive to others' feelings and expectations and inspires teamwork.

'Drive' style requires the ability to move between 'Head', 'Heart' and 'Feet', to be able to adjust your personal style according to the changing needs of the situation.

Personal Development Toolkit

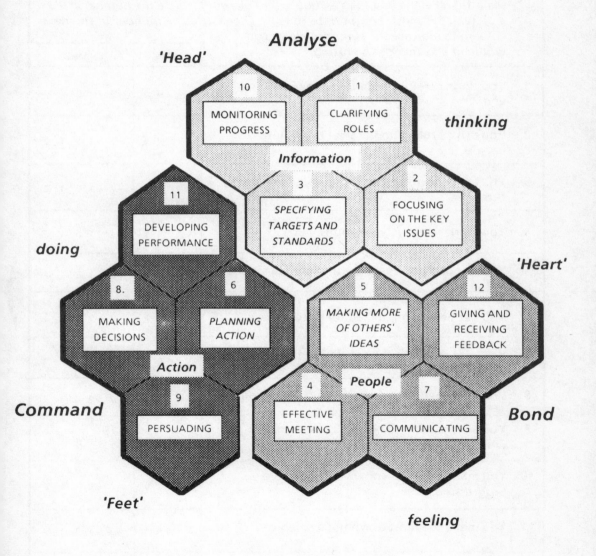

Style Questionnaire

3.1 Score the extent to which the following statements apply to you NOW on a scale 1–5 (1 = Not you; 3 = Yes, but...; 5 = Fully you). Circle the number (1 2 3 4 5) which is most appropriate to you. Then circle the number in the next column to indicate the extent to which you would like to change this rating:

	'NOW'	'CHANGE'
1. You think carefully about what needs doing and why.	1 2 **3** 4 5	+2 +1 **0** -1 -2
2. You can be relied upon to get things into perspective.	1 2 **3** 4 5	+2 **+1** 0 -1 -2
3. You are concerned that things should be done correctly.	1 2 3 4 **5**	+2 +1 0 **-1** -2
4. You work effectively in groups.	1 2 **3** 4 5	**+2** +1 0 -1 -2
5. You respond positively to other people's ideas.	1 2 3 **4** 5	+2 **+1** 0 -1 -2
6. You get people organized for action.	1 2 3 **4** 5	+2 **+1** 0 -1 -2
7. You consistently keep people informed.	1 2 3 **4** 5	+2 **+1** 0 -1 -2
8. You have no difficulty making up your mind.	1 2 3 **4** 5	+2 **+1** 0 -1 -2
9. You always seem to be able to get others to do what you want.	1 2 3 **4** 5	**+2** +1 0 -1 -2
10. You make sure you know how things are progressing.	1 2 3 **4** 5	+2 **+1** 0 -1 -2
11. You make the most of what is available.	1 2 3 **4** 5	+2 **+1** 0 -1 -2
12. You prefer to deal with people face-to-face.	1 **2** 3 4 5	**+2** +1 0 -1 -2

Bold type represents the scores in the example on page 35.   © PETER GRAINGER 1994

3.2   To consider your own relationship to the three basic styles transfer your *'Now'* scores and the *'Change'* scores from the questionnaire according to the number of each statement. Add up the total *'Now'* scores and note down the most significant *'Change'* scores, keeping the two sets separate:

	'NOW' SCORES	'CHANGE' SCORES

'Analyse'

1. You think carefully about what needs doing and why.   [   ] *4*   [   ] *0*

3. You are concerned that things should be done correctly.   [   ] *5*   [   ] *-1*

10. You make sure you know how things are progressing.   [   ] *4*   [   ] *+1*

2. You can be relied upon to get things into perspective.   [   ] *4*   [   ] *+1*

TOTAL   [   ] *17*

'Bond'

7. You consistently keep people informed.   [   ] *4*   [   ] *+1*

12. You prefer to deal with people face-to-face.   [   ] *2*   [(+2)]

5. You respond positively to other people's ideas.   [   ] *3*   [   ] *+1*

4. You work effectively in groups.   [   ] *3*   [(+2)]

TOTAL   [   ] *12*

'Command'

9. You always seem to be able to get others to do what you want.   [   ] *3*   [(+2)]

6. You get people organized for action.   [   ] *4*   [   ] *+1*

8. You have no difficulty making up your mind.   [   ] *3*   [   ] *+1*

11. You make the most of what is available.   [   ] *4*   [   ] *+1*

TOTAL   [   ] *14*

Example scores are in **bold type**; the resulting profile appears on Page 35.

4. Style profile

You should now have a total score for each style, but these totals do not tell you very much until you see them graphically in relation to each other. It is this inter-relationship that is important, not the size of the totals produced.

By transferring your total scores for 'Analyse', 'Bond' and 'Command' on to the model on page 37 your profile will normally emerge as a triangle with a 'pull' towards one particular area of skills .

In the example opposite the person's *strengths* lie at the top towards 'Analyse'. The skills in that area are 'monitoring progress', 'clarifying roles' and 'specifying targets and standards'. The area on the *opposite* side to the shape of the profile (shaded) covers skills from BA to CB. These are likely to be among the skills to concentrate on as personal development priorities. 'Making more of others' ideas' and giving and receiving feedback' are of course covered in this workbook.

If the triangle of your profile is equilateral you are probably 'Drive' style, or at least have the potential to be. But it is more likely that there will be a 'pull' in one particular direction, a 'skew' towards one style or perhaps two. This skew will be in the direction of your *natural* strengths, and the skills on the model *nearest* to that skew will identify a particular area of confidence and competence for you.

Example of Completed Style Profile

4.1 Write your total 'Now' scores for each 'style' from 3.2 on page 33 in the boxes below:

'Analyse':   'Bond':   'Command':

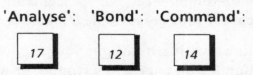

17   12   14

Circle or cross the appropriate number on the model below, and join up the points to produce a style profile. Then highlight the skills with the highest 'Change' scores:

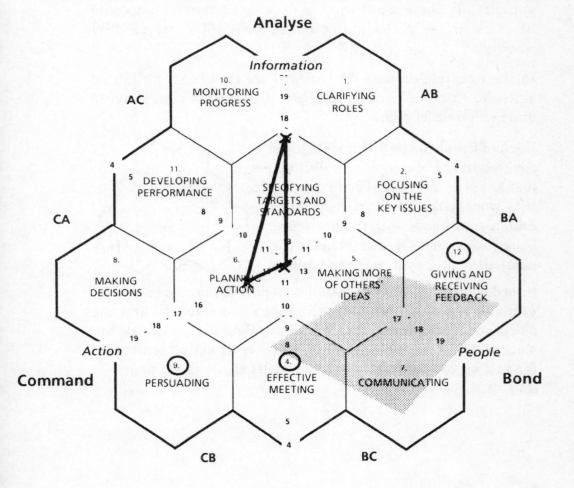

The skills on the model *furthest away* from the shape of your profile are those that you probably do not find easy to carry out; you may therefore need to concentrate on them particularly as part of your personal development.

To check out your priorities, highlight your highest 'Change' scores from Section 3.2 on page 33 by ringing or underlining the appropriate number on the model opposite. These may be skills which you find difficult and want to improve or skills you already possess but want to develop further. (They could be +2s or +1s depending on the overall level of your scoring.)

In the example on page 35 you will see that the highlighted skills (ie +2s) are 'persuading', 'effective meeting' and 'giving and receiving feedback'.

Each of the skills in the model opposite is covered in the Manager's Toolkit series, just as skills 5, 11 and 12 are covered in this workbook. You can therefore match your needs with the particular book in the series which includes the particular skills you want to acquire.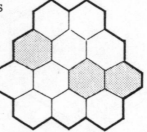

In order to focus on your own development plan, it is helpful to make a note of the strengths that have emerged and the skills you find difficult that you now intend to concentrate on. You will find suitable formats, which will act as reminders for you as you move through the skills sections, on pages 38 and 39.

Style Profile

4.2 Write your total 'Now' scores for each 'style' from 3.2 on page 33 in the boxes below:

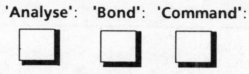

'Analyse':   'Bond':   'Command':

Circle or cross the appropriate number on the model below, and join up the points to produce a style profile. Then highlight the skills with the highest 'Change' scores:

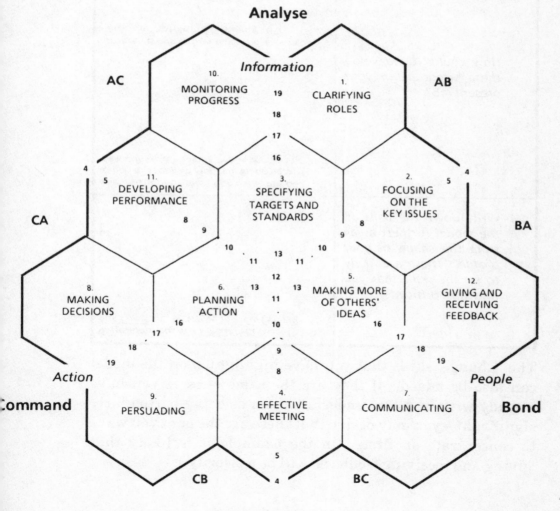

© PETER GRAINGER 1994

From consideration of your profile, identify your strongest skills in the space below and consider ways of developing them. Then make a note of the skills furthest away from the shape of your profile, and confirm that these are the skills you want to improve.

4.3 Write down the skills closest to the shape of your profile. These are likely to be your natural strengths: How could you develop these strengths in your present job?	*Monitoring progress, clarifying roles and specifying targets and standards* *Ensure everyone knows what they're supposed to be doing and how well they're doing. Perhaps coach other managers in the skills*
4.4 Write down the skills on the model furthest away from the shape of your profile. These are likely to be the skills that you find most difficult:	*Making more of others' ideas, giving and receiving feedback and communicating*

The 'Change' skills that you have highlighted on the model can also be added. If they are the same ones as you have already written down, underline them as being particularly significant – you may decide that these are the ones you want to concentrate on first. (In the example it is likely that 'giving and receiving feedback' will be a priority.)

> 4.4 (continued) *Add the high-lighted 'Change' skills, underlining any on page 38 that are the same:*
>
> *How committed are you to improving these skills?*
>
>   *Effective meeting and persuading*
>
>
>   *If I want to be an effective manager I've got to be able get people to do what I want, face-to-face and in groups*

5. Career profile

Just as our personal style influences the way we perform certain management skills, so style affects our suitability for one type of career rather than another. By distributing a sample of career types around the Personal Development Toolkit according to the appropriateness of each style, it is possible to link the shape of a style profile with certain types of career.

The model on page 40 contains only examples, and in no way represents the range of careers available. It does, however, suggest that there are 'information', 'people' and 'action' types of careers, which may suit 'Analyse', 'Bond' and 'Command' types of people.

The model is offered as a further way of looking at career and personal development options. But do remember that as one progresses in a particular career, the style differences between careers gradually disappear, and the balanced management/leadership requirements of 'Drive' style become increasingly important (see page 30).

There are, of course, numerous career guidance aids, and, because we are not dealing with an exact science, no single aid is going to provide the ideal guide. It is a matter of trying a number of information aids, and looking for a *trend towards* one type of career in which you are likely to realize your potential, and *away* from others which are unlikely to suit your talents. View this model as another coordinate against which to check the direction of your personal development.

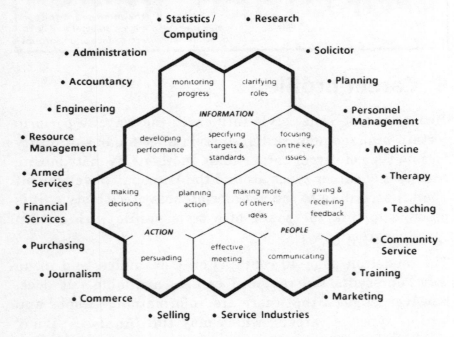

The 'People' skills, with explanations on the left and practice activities on the right, now follow. In the development activities in Chapter Three, remember that you can have *your own* personal development in mind, or the development of a particular individual – inside or outside the working environment.

Chapter Two

MAKING MORE OF OTHERS' IDEAS

Chapter Two

MAKING MORE
OF OTHERS' IDEAS

Making more of others' ideas helps you to develop other people's
potential for creativity.

1. Encouraging

Generally speaking we are not very good at encouraging
other people's ideas. We like our own ideas of course, but are
strangely suspicious of those contributed by other people.
And yet creativity, particularly in a group, is one sure way of
bringing about new solutions to old problems.

If we are going to want ideas from other people it is important
that we help to create an environment and an atmosphere in
which ideas are positively encouraged. Everyone attending a
meeting can actively encourage a positive atmosphere in the
way they behave. Certain interpersonal skills are particularly helpful; for example, checking that you have really
understood what someone else has just said.

If the group from which you want ideas is reluctant to make
suggestions, it may be necessary to get the flow of ideas going
by making the first suggestions yourself and trying to get
some reaction to them. Sometimes someone who has been
very quiet needs to be brought into the discussion and will
then contribute an excellent idea, because he or she has
actually been listening carefully to what has been said.

1. Encouraging

Are the meetings you attend short of ideas or new approaches to old problems?

1.1 *Think of a meeting or an item on the agenda of a meeting when ideas are particularly going to be needed:*	*Ideas on how to reduce costs by 7%*
1.2 *How can you help to create an environment in which people will be encouraged to give ideas?* *How do you personally encourage others' ideas?*	*A brief break, special and fun; stress I do need their ideas*
1.3 *Would making the ideas visible (eg writing them on a flipchart or marker board) help?* *If so, how could you make a board available?*	*Flipchart is essential - ask Jane to arrange*

If you want specifically to encourage a flow of ideas, try to get the group to relax. Demonstrate a relaxed style yourself and try to make the experience enjoyable. Limit the clarification of each idea to a basic understanding so that the flow does not get bogged down in a mass of unnecessary and detailed information.

Above all stop people criticizing each other's ideas, at least initially. There is no surer way to stop people contributing than to have others say 'It won't work', 'It'll cost too much' etc, and yet that is the normal response to ideas. We seem to pride ourselves in being able to shoot down another person's idea, or at least to analyse it until all the life has drained out of it.

2. Responding

Supposing suggestions are generally slow to be made, the flow does not gather pace and the discussion seems flat. Often the cause of this is a lack of response, nobody is *reacting* to what others are saying. They may have drifted into a clarifying mode, providing plenty of *information*, but there is no feeling and no excitement.

Positive responses – 'Great idea!' – are very helpful, yet we rarely make them. Even disagreement can stimulate creativity on occasions, provided we trust the motives; it is seen to be helping the group to move forward. At least we know where we are if somebody disagrees.

But it is essential that disagreement never becomes personal, when the criticism is directed at the *person* who made the suggestion rather than the idea itself. What matters most is some form of *reaction*, producing urgency and energy to help trigger further outbursts of mental creativity.

2. Responding

How good are you at responding to other people and their ideas?

2.1 Write down the last occasion you expressed your feelings about something or someone:	*When Jane gave in her notice*
2.2 When was the last occasion you expressed support for another person's idea?	*When Marketing suggested a major client we had missed*
2.3 If you recently disagreed with an idea, was it clear to others why you disagreed? Did your disageement become personal or emotional?	*David's office layout proposal - we'd only just settled in!*

2.4 Identify two people you know who might be termed 'low reactors'. Consider how far they match each of the following characteristics:

	NAME A:	B:
You never know what they are thinking, let alone feeling.		
They always seem to give the impression of disagreement and disapproval.		
I feel myself talking too much and over-reacting when I meet them.		
Personal relationships seem to be awkward and forced for no apparent reason.		

It is at this point that the 'low reactor' is encountered. 'Low reactors' are people who do not want to – or do not know how to – show their feelings. Because they do not respond, it is assumed that they are disapproving and disagreeing, when often the reverse is the case.

In order to get some response from low reactors people are inclined to talk more than they should and to over-react. It is difficult to build up a relationship with a low reactor, often for no apparent reason. It seems that *we all need feedback* of some kind, and if we don't get it we tend to suspect the worst.

Low reactors can also adversely affect teamwork and creativity. With little or no response from members of the group ideas gradually dry up or never emerge in the first place. People will not know what is wrong and the pace will consequently get slower and slower, the atmosphere less and less stimulating.

The person whose profile appears in the 'Personal style' section, for example, is probably a 'low reactor' (see page 35). He thinks he works effectively in groups, but could actually be limiting the creativity of the meetings he attends by lack of response.

Asking questions, particularly about feelings, can help. 'How do you feel about that, Jim?' In extreme cases, a personal response, like 'Are you really saying you couldn't care less, Jim?' can open things up. But it has to be handled with great care to avoid a series of knock-on personal attacks or, more likely, switching the person off from contributing completely.

Similarly a *high* reactor can also be 'controlled' by *asking questions* – factual questions, not about feelings – or by checking the meaning behind the reactions that have been revealed.

	A	B
2.4 (continued) What is the effect of each of these two people on a group?	*Never wants to get involved*	*Slows us all down*
Could other people see you in this way?	*I don't think so - I tend to let everyone know how I feel!*	
2.5 Questioning and checking help to counter the effect of the low and high reactor. How good are you at these skills? Think of an occasion when they would have been useful in this way:	*When Brian went on about not enough time for full discussion - I forget when short of time or frustrated*	

3. Brainstorming

Do you have you a particular problem which could benefit from the application of new ideas?

3.1 Write down the situation that you want to put right or improve:

Customers are not paying on time

3.   Brainstorming

The technique of 'brainstorming' now seems to have entered everyday conversation as a means of getting people to think creatively. It would be as well to remind ourselves of what is actually involved, because it is not as easy to apply as is often supposed.

First, the atmosphere must be relaxed, undisturbed and as much fun as possible.   A flipchart or marker-board is essential, with a scribe who writes quickly but fairly legibly at the ready.   It is very important to write at the top of the flipchart the purpose of the brainstorming session, preferably as a 'how to' statement, so that you get ideas for *action* (for example, 'How to persuade customer X to pay on time').

The secret of successful brainstorming is to use it sparingly on very specific and focused problems – or parts of a problem – which cannot be solved in any other way. By keeping the issue focused and precise, the spread of free-flowing ideas will be limited by the *precision* of the clarification that takes place *before* the flow of ideas is asked for. It is like pouring ideas into a flask – the neck of the flask must be carefully defined before pouring begins.

Many people know that brainstorming is about *not evaluating any* of the ideas that come from the group; but it is also essential not to *clarify* any idea – that can be done at the building stage. Indeed it is important *actively* to encourage ideas, particularly from those – 'Analyse' people probably! – who may not be comfortable with such a free-for-all process.

Every idea *must* go up on the board, however seemingly irrelevant, and even if it has come up before.   The idea's juxtaposition with others at a different time will frequently

3.1 (continued) Rewrite what you have just written as a precise 'How to' statement which describes what the ideas are to achieve in order to put the situation right:

How to persuade Customer X to pay our monthly invoice within 28 days

3.2 It is possible to practise brainstorming on your own. Take a sheet of A4 paper and write what you have written above at the top of the sheet.

Now think of any idea – however impractical or crazy – that could achieve what you have written, and write it on the sheet of paper. DO NOT evaluate or filter out ANY of your ideas.

How to persuade Customer X to pay our monthly invoice within 28 days.

1 Offer incentive	13 Build relationship
2 Get rid of them	14 Show effect
3 Telephone	15 Press campaign
4 Advertise	16 Get the facts!
5 Rogue's gallery	17 Do _they_ have poor payers?
6 Why worry?	18 Show costs
7 Ask Chamber of C.	19 Charge interest
8 Ask Institute	20 Delay delivery
9 Ask them!	21 Cash on delivery
10 Read a book	22 Ask other companies
11 Go on a course	23 Make a video
12 Who pays now?	24 Have fun!

Number the ideas on your sheet of paper so that you can put them into appropriate 'boxes'.

3.3 Look through your list of ideas and write down five or six headings under which you can group the ideas:

Put the appropriate numbers in each 'box':

A	B
ADVERSE PUBLICITY: 4, 5, 15	GET KNOW-HOW: 7, 8, 10, 11, 22
C	**D**
PENALTIES ON THEM: 2, 19, 20, 21	TALK TO THEM: 3, 9, 13, 17, 23, 24
E	
IMPACT ON US?: 6, 12, 14, 16, 18	

trigger a totally different range of thoughts. Sometimes it is worthwhile to throw in apparently unrelated ideas or even really crazy thoughts to stimulate different associations in individuals' minds – humour can work wonders!

Brainstorming is like a laser beam and needs to be handled carefully and accurately to gain maximum benefit. Sessions should therefore be very short – between five and ten minutes – to maintain the energy and enjoyment levels. If you arrange a number of short focused sessions, the *second and third* will be the most productive, as the group gets into its stride but before it tires.

Often people do not know how to handle the bulk of ideas that usually results. One group produced 140 ideas in under ten minutes! It has been known for leaders of brainstorming sessions to pick just one or two feasible ideas from the list and ignore the rest. Why, then, bother with brainstorming?

I have regularly proved that *every idea from a brainstorming session can be used*. First, number each idea, however crazy it seems, and then try to create about six 'boxes' on a flipchart into which the numbered ideas can be put. The headings need not be very precise because they are only for bringing associated ideas together.

20, 24, 28, 29	1, 3, 4, 14, 25, 27, 30
8, 9, 11, 16, 17, 22	15, 21, 23, 31
2, 7, 12, 15, 16, 19, 26	5, 6, 10, 18, 30

Members of the group can save time by each taking a box and filling it with numbered ideas appropriate to that heading. When the appropriate numbers are in each box, they can be converted back into ideas, and built together to create elements of a draft plan (see 'building' overleaf). This step can work particularly well with pairs sharing ideas and building phrases into a plan together.

3.4 Now write the ideas in an appropriate order on a sheet of paper, trying to build each into action steps to improve the situation described in 3.1.	*1. Quantify the impact of late payment on us, the size of the problem, who pays on time and who doesn't. Is it really that serious? (E)* *2. Develop personal and telephone contacts with the customer, building a closer and more relaxed relationship. Be in a position to explain the problem, illustrating the impact of the problem on us. Ask if they have a similar problem and, if so, how do <u>they</u> deal with it? (D)* *3. Find out how other Cos deal with late payment via Chamber of Commerce, Institute, publications, other companies and perhaps attending a training course (B).* *4. If the situation is serious, consider joining small business campaign against late payment, involving local press and identifying customer locally (A).* *5. Consider penalty options, eg charging interest, COD, delayed delivery or even withdrawing supplies (C).*
3.5 You have now gone through the process yourself. Would you like a group to tackle this problem? If so, when would you like them to meet and who will arrange it? Is there another issue which would benefit from brainstorming? If there is, how will you make it happen?	*Yes. By end of May - I'll arrange at next team meeting* *I'll ask team and handle at same session*

4. Building

How good are you personally at developing other people's ideas?

4.1 Identify the last idea that anyone put to you.	*David's* *point about finding out what other sections were doing*

4. Building

To be able to build on another person's idea you need to check your understanding of what has just been said – or written. You cannot build if you have not listened to or do not understand what has just been said. If you do not like the idea, look for the specific *element* you do not like rather than throwing out the concept as a whole. If I suggest we take an idea to our boss, for example, instead of rejecting the proposal by saying 'You can never get hold of him', you might suggest we catch him after tomorrow's team meeting. You have accepted the need to talk to the boss, but have solved the problem of his availability by suggesting a time which overcomes that weakness.

'Patching flaws', as the technique is called, tries to prevent the air escaping through the puncture that someone's adverse comment has made in the balloon of the idea. For some reason most of us seem to enjoy trying to destroy other people's ideas. Patching flaws diverts people's creativity away from shooting ideas down to thinking of ways of overcoming the weakness that may have been identified.

If patching flaws doesn't work with particularly negative people, ask them to think of three things that they actually *like* about the idea. By the time they have thought of the three positive things, the previous objections have largely disappeared. For an intelligent person who enjoys killing others' suggestions, it can become an intellectual challenge he or she cannot resist! If handled creatively at meetings it can also prove valuable learning for the group as a whole – *and* they will probably enjoy it! If a group is having fun it is probably also being creative – and vice versa.

4.1 (continued) Can you remember if you check- ed your understanding of the full meaning of the suggestion?	*No! I assumed he was 'having a go'!*
4.2 If it was an unrealistic suggestion, what was your objection to it? Try to think of a way of overcoming that object- ion without rejecting the whole idea.	*It would be seen as competitive* *See it as sharing for good of Dept as a whole - let them have ours*
4.3 If the idea still seems to have no merit, see if you can think of three things you like about it. Do you think the idea has any more merit now?	1. *Encourages dialogue* 2. *Broader perspective* 3. *Boss will like it* *Yes!*
4.4 Take that idea or any other that you can recall being offered and try to build on it, ie develop it, make it more effective and useful.	*Open list of ideas for whole Dept; a 'Competition' for best ideas*

IDEAS QUESTIONNAIRE

Think back to the last meeting (or part of a meeting) you attended at which ideas were needed and consider how effective you were at encouraging and developing them:

Interpersonal Skills:

How effective do think you were in using these inter-personal skills?
 	
Score: 'H' (too much use)
       'M' (about right)
       'L' (too little use)
	TITLE & DATE OF MEETING:
	
	Team Meeting, 10 June 1994
	
	QUESTIONING [L] RESPONDING [L]
	
	CHECKING [L] BUILDING [M]

Making More of Others' Ideas:

1.	How far did you help to create an environment in which people were encouraged to give ideas?	*I didn't make the break in the meeting that I had planned. My commitment to their ideas was constrained by time and the 'ideas' item coming at the end of a long meeting.*
	Were the ideas made visible?	*We had a flipchart and wrote ideas up as they came, but there weren't many.*
2.	How much responding was there at the meeting? How open were people with their feelings and concerns?	*That was the trouble – you didn't really know what people were thinking, let alone feeling. The ideas just didn't seem to flow...*
	Were there any 'high' or 'low reactors' present and if so, how did you deal with them?	*I think they all must have been 'low reactors' – except Brian! I lost interest myself after a while. I'll try asking them for their reactions to ideas next time.*

3.	Did you try brainstorming, or consider its use? If not, why not? If you did use it, how successful were you?	*No – atmosphere was all wrong. I suppose it might have livened things up if I had made it a special session. I felt there wasn't time, but it didn't need to take long and it was an important subject.*
4.	If you considered some ideas unrealistic, did you a. check your understanding of them? b. explain your specific objection and try to overcome the objection? c. reject the idea as a whole?	*No – I felt pressure of time and didn't give it proper thought.* *I didn't like Brian's suggestion that we split the agenda into two meetings, but I didn't explain.* *It would actually have helped me overcome the time pressure. I was determined at least to make a start on ideas for cost reduction.*
5.	Do you remember expressing support for a particular idea? Did you or anyone else try to build on it?	*Yes – the idea of going direct to individuals who were keen. Perhaps we could get them all together some time (brainstorm?).* *Yes – Jane developed it further by suggesting we could get their ideas on a regular basis along with the monthly figures.*
6.	Did any disagreements during the meeting become personal or emotional?	*Not really, although Jim went very quiet after Brian said the delay was typical of 'his friends in Finance'. He could have 'had a go' at him later.*

IDEAS QUESTIONNAIRE

Think back to the last meeting (or part of a meeting) you attended at which ideas were needed and consider how effective you were at encouraging and developing them:

Interpersonal Skills:

How effective do think you were in using these inter-personal skills? Score: 'H' (too much use) 'M' (about right) 'L' (too little use)	TITLE & DATE OF MEETING:
	QUESTIONING ☐ RESPONDING ☐ CHECKING ☐ BUILDING ☐

Making More of Others' Ideas:

1. How far did you help to create an environment in which people were encouraged to give ideas? Were the ideas made visible?	
2. How much responding was there at the meeting? How open were people with their feelings and concerns? Were there any 'high' or 'low reactors' present and if so, how did you deal with them?	

3. Did you try brainstorming, or consider its use? If not, why not? If you did use it, how successful were you?	

4. If you considered some ideas unrealistic, did you
 	
  a. check your understanding of them?
 	
  b. explain your specific objection and try to overcome the objection?
 	
  c. reject the idea as a whole?	

5. Do you remember expressing support for a particular idea? Did you or anyone else try to build on it?	
6. Did any disagreements during the meeting become personal or emotional?	

Making More of Other's Ideas
links to other skills in
the Manager's Toolkit series

Each skill in this workbook not only links directly with other 'people' skills in the workbook (12), but also with other skills from the toolkit on page 13 (1, 2, 4, and 6).

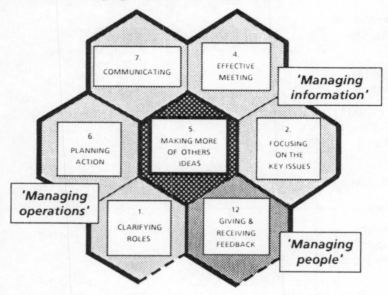

When planning individual roles (1) or team action plans (6) a positive response to others' ideas is essential, not only to broaden the range of options but also to encourage commitment.

In 'managing information' others' ideas can throw up additional factors, as well as new solutions, when focusing on key issues (2). Having meetings (4) without recognizing and developing the ideas of the members of the group will soon become sterile, while effective communicating (7) with your team necessitates being willing to accept their suggestions for improving performance.

Chapter Three

DEVELOPING PERFORMANCE

Chapter Three

DEVELOPING PERFORMANCE

Developing performance provides you with the means to make the most of your own and your team members' personal and career potential.

1. Creating the environment

If we are going to develop the performance and potential of those who work for us we have to create an environment in which improvement and development are actively encouraged. We have to behave in a manner which anticipates those around us taking chances with what they do in order to extend their repertoire of skills.

Demonstrating the Pygmalion Effect in the way we manage (see pages 24–7), showing that we *expect* people to stretch themselves and to succeed in what they attempt, will help enormously in giving people confidence to 'have a go'. The example we set, the trust we demonstrate, the confidence we project to each individual is critical to success.

This means treating everyone the same, the least effective performer in your department, as well the best. Often we *behave* differently towards the people we expect little from. We are likely to have less contact with poor performers, to have lower expectations of what they can achieve, and, lo and behold, they perform less well and we have created a self-fulfilling prophecy.

1. Creating the environment

Does your behaviour as a manager affect the performance and development of your staff?

1.1 *Think of the most effective member of your staff (or the person not in your section with whom you work best). How do you behave towards him or her?*	*Jim: relaxed and encouraging, frequent informal contacts*
1.2 *Think of the least effective member of your staff (or the person not in your section with whom you have most difficulty working). How do you behave towards him or her?*	*Margaret: I avoid her, and am on edge, in case there's hassle*
1.3 *Compare your behaviour towards the two people. How far is any difference the result of your different expectations of each of them?*	*I expect J to perform well and M to be difficult - it happens!*
1.4 *How might your behaviour towards either of them be changed to better effect?*	*More informal contact with M, smile, show interest in job*

One way to make sure that you do at least try to treat your staff in the same way, is to discuss their performance with each of them *one-to-one on a regular basis.* Everyone deserves to know how well they are perceived to be performing, and to receive personal feedback from the person responsible for their job performance.

Meaningful individual feedback, which we shall look at in depth in the next chapter, can only come from a regular, two-way discussion – at least bi-monthly – in which real dialogue about personal and work targets takes place in the context of agreed longer-term personal development.

Discussion about personal and career development is so often omitted because of lack of discussion time, lack of thinking time or fear of losing the person concerned. An exceptional performer is likely to move on anyway if no development plans are made, and everyone's day-to-day performance is enhanced if they believe their manager is genuinely interested in their long-term future. A company or department with a reputation for developing its people attracts both talent and potential – and vice versa.

2. Auditing talents

One way of gaining confidence in the process of developing individuals is to start with yourself. If you can think through a development plan for yourself, preparing one with another person will be much less daunting (*MCI Unit 5*).

The open learning approach of the Toolkit series is about self development, taking action to acquire and improve skills as a result of your own efforts. The performance of those skills is significantly affected by the type of person you are, and so it is important to understand yourself and your personal style.

1.5 How often do you talk over their performance with individual members of your staff? Is this usually done by means of an informal one-to-one discussion in an office or quiet place?	
	Once in 6 wks - usually interrupted or linked to meetings
1.6 Do you have an annual (or more frequent) appraisal with each member of your staff? Does this more formal performance review provide an opportunity to discuss training and development needs?	
	Yes *But we tend to run out of time before in depth discussion*

2. Auditing talents

Are you clear on your own personal and career development needs for the foreseeable future?

2.1 From your own style profile and the conclusions on page 39, make a note of your strengths and the skills you find most difficult:

Have these been confirmed by other people?

Strengths	Limitations
Getting things done, leadership, under pressure	*Impatience with people, more time to think - boss confirmed at appraisal*

In the Personal Development section of each of the books in the Toolkit series you will come across the *style questionnaire and profile*, with different profile examples demonstrated in each book. This is an appropriate place to begin considering development needs. By considering your own style profile – and later other people's – you will become aware of the strengths which need to 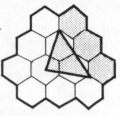 be exploited and the limitations which need to be overcome.

You can reinforce the picture of yourself that emerges from your style profile by completing an audit of your achievements and points of enjoyment. By looking back on all the things you have been *consistently good at* in your life – and it is a question of looking at your *life*, rather than just your working career – you will create a kaleidoscope of achievement, focused in contrast to your areas of consistent non-achievement.

If you then add all the things you have consistently *enjoyed*, however apparently insignificant they may seem, plus all the things you have *never* enjoyed, you will have a picture of yourself based on *evidence* to place beside your style profile. Enjoyment represents motivation, activities over which you are likely to be enthusiastic, and self-motivation and enthusiasm are, of course, critical to effective development.

On page 40 you will find the Career Profile which suggests the type of career with which a person with a certain profile bias is likely to be most comfortable. Look at your profile in relation to the types of career represented around the outside of the model. Is a consistent picture emerging, a career direction resulting from the various sources which convinces you of the way you should be moving?

2.2 List below on the left all the types of things you have been consistently good
at all your life, and on the right all the types of things that you have never
been good at. (You may know of someone else who could do the same.)

Things I have been consistently good at:	Things I have consistently <u>not</u> been good at:
Climbing, selling, rugby, tennis, building walls	*Exams, paperwork, systems, DIY, crosswords*

2.3 Now list on the left the types of things that you have always enjoyed doing,
and on the right the types of things that you have never enjoyed doing.

Things I have consistently enjoyed doing:	Things I have never enjoyed doing:
All sports, parties, challenges, competition, travel	*Routines, reading, umpiring, budgets, appraisal*

2.4 From an analysis of Sections 2.1–2.3 and a look at your career profile on
page 40, note down the type of work or career in which you are most likely
to do well:

Challenging, including leading others, pressure, variety and an out-of-doors content

If you are satisfied with the coordinated picture that emerges, consider what you need to *do* to help you along the path outlined. And what help as coach or mentor could other people, especially your manager, give you? Do you need specific skills to plug a gap? Are you going to need particular experience in an area? If so how are you going to acquire it without upsetting the smooth running of the departments concerned?

3. Planning development

Analysing your own career will not only enable you to experience the various profiling tools, but give you a chance to *visualize* a plan, the steps or objectives by which you may be able to move from where you are now to where you want to be. It is a creative as well as an analytical process, and visualizing situations and experiences, as well as utilizing available resources, requires imagination and practice.

Creating a plan is determining *who* is to do *what* by *when*, so that you have a sequence of steps and priorities. (See 'Planning Action' in Volume 1, *Managing Operations*.) What is the critical step for you to make, when should you have made it by, and whose help is going to be essential to that step?

As you consider all these factors for yourself, it is only a short step to do the same for members of your *team*. But remember not everyone needs – or indeed wants – to be developed. Some may be quite happy carrying out a routine job and would find it stressful to have more responsibility. Others may get their challenge in life from activities outside their work.

However, I would suggest many more people would benefit from personal development attention than are receiving it

2.5	What action to help you to develop is needed by yourself? by someone else?	
		Consciously try to use checking behaviour and 'count to ten!' *Ask for feedback from team on listening - and patience!*

3. Planning development

Do you want to improve your ability to develop yourself, your staff and your team as a whole?

3.1	From your conclusions in Section 2 above, write a personal plan for you to follow in order to make the most of your potential:	
		Complete and practise Managing People; *help from staff in listening and paperwork; discuss career with boss in 6 mths' time*
3.2	Identify one member of your staff who needs to acquire or develop a specific skill: How far can you help by coaching him or her individually? How far could other members of the team help with coaching?	
		Brian doesn't listen - explain and demonstrate at meetings *Team could help at meetings when he doesn't, keep it fun*

at the present time. The very act of being able to discuss it with their manager from time to time – that he or she has actually given it some thought – would have an immediate impact on their attitude and their performance.

Try to see the development process as a *team* activity. The team can have as dramatic an effect on a person's performance and development as their manager. They can create or destroy a learning environment, and the balance of the personal styles within the team can prove critical. Consider the styles of your staff or the people you work with. Do you have a spread of 'Analyse', 'Bond' and 'Command', and, if not, what is the effect of the imbalance on their working relationships?

Think of those who would benefit most from development activity, especially those who have particular talent and potential, and whose performance is likely to fall off if you do not take action.

Be creative about development opportunities. Do you let them cover all or part of your work when you are on holiday? Is there a special project you need doing which would give them the specific experience they need? Could they be released to another department for a month or two to gain particular expertise, or perhaps exchange with someone needing experience with you? A lateral move (ie one without promotion) is often beneficial and is a good test of the genuineness of a person's commitment to development.

And if you still can't bring yourself to take action which may result in the premature departure of one of your best workers, try to be creative about how you might replace them – it provides an excellent opportunity to practise brainstorming from the previous chapter!

3.3 Consider the styles of the key members of your team and make a note of them as letters (see page 35):

Name 1: Jim   style: AB

Name 2: Brian   style: AC

Name 3: Margaret   style: A

Name 4: Jane   style: BC

Do their styles help to explain why they get on well or not so well?

Complementary styles - M as 'Analyse' remote from team

Is there anything you could do to improve their personal relation- ships or the effective- ness of the team?

Involve M more in team and ask Jane to aid teamwork

3.4 Think of one of your staff who could benefit from development. Consider how far each of the following could be valuable experience:

As holiday cover:	Internal project:
Jim: Cover part of my work while I'm on holiday	Cost Project sufficient challenge at present
Temporary assignment:	Lateral move:
Sales experience to widen vision	Could do Brian's job in a year's time

3.5 If this person were to move as part of their development, how could you cover their work?

Try brainstorming alternatives:

Promote Jane, split work, M grow into it?, Finance help...

DEVELOPING WORKSHEET

Identify one of your staff who is seeking personal and/or career development. Plan what action he or she and you need to take, and arrange to talk it over face-to-face. If you are not currently responsible for the development of such a person, complete the worksheet for *yourself*.

NAME: *Jim Cunningham*	DATE OF PLANNED DISCUSSION: *5 June 1994*
1. If you have discussed his or her development on a previous occasion, what ACTION did you agree then, and how much has been carried out?	*Jim had only been with us for nine months at his last appraisal. He was still getting to know how the department worked, but I did specially ask him to develop good relations with Finance, which he's done with some success.*
2. Think about the person's PERFORMANCE of both the targets and the routine activities of his or her job:	*Jim is always looking for new ways of doing things, has plenty of ideas himself, but is inclined to forget to take others along with him. Is a valuable information source for the department, and has developed good relations with other departments so that we get cooperation from them, especially Finance.*
Try to summarize your conclusions on the person's overall STRENGTHS AND LIMITATIONS that emerge:	*I think he prefers setting up systems and procedures rather than keeping them going, so he must learn to delegate and to monitor results on a regular basis. I'm not yet sure how he copes with pressure.*
3. Consider the person's personal STYLE and any information you have about his or her career ASPIRATIONS: Does the corresponding CAREER PROFILE on page 40 help to confirm the development picture?	*He is an 'Analyse/Bond' person who is very logical and systematic, but who is concerned to get the best out of people. I know he wants to be a manager, although it has been too early to discuss formally till now. In a couple more years as he develops his man management skills (and his patience!) he will make an effective manager. His profile confirms a planning/service role.*

4.	What actions need to be taken to help overcome his or her LIMITATIONS?	*He could benefit from working through* Managing People. *He should learn to talk to colleagues more informally, in a more relaxed, less intense manner.*
	by him/herself:	
	by coaching from you:	*We can share open learning experiences, as together we learn patience and to listen! I will talk over the problem with Margaret with him, and check that he keeps others with him on the Cost Control project. I will monitor his deadlines closely for next month.*
	by help from someone else (incl. off-the-job training):	*Members of department can provide feedback – tactfully!*
	specific work experience:	*Chairing team meetings for relevant items.*
5.	What action needs to be taken to help the person develop his or her STRENGTHS AND POTENTIAL?	*Cover for me when I'm away.* *Project with Sales to broaden perspective.*
	internal project/experience:	*Finance management may be interested in his aspirations and helping with his development.*
	external assignment:	*He will need off-the-job management training in about 18 mths.*
	lateral move/ promotion:	
6.	Prepare a draft DEVELOPMENT PLAN which takes note of the help above, and which you can discuss with the person when you meet at the agreed date:	*1. We'll resolve problem with Margaret in one month.* *2. We'll watch team meeting agendas for suitable items for chairing practice and review.* *3. I'll monitor Cost Control project every two weeks until progress is assured; review results with Jim.* *4. Jim will work through* Managing People *Sept–Oct and discuss progress/experience with me.* *5. Look out for suitable project with Sales in six mths.* *6. Review management training needs at appraisal.*

DEVELOPING WORKSHEET

Identify one of your staff who is seeking personal and/or career development. Plan what action he or she and you need to take, and arrange to talk it over face-to-face. If you are not currently responsible for the development of such a person, complete the worksheet for *yourself*.

NAME:	DATE OF PLANNED DISCUSSION:
1. If you have discussed his or her development on a previous occasion, what ACTION did you agree then, and how much has been carried out?	
2. Think about the person's PERFORMANCE of both the targets and the routine activities of his or her job: Try to summarize your conclusions on the person's overall STRENGTHS AND LIMITATIONS that emerge:	
3. Consider the person's personal STYLE and any information you have about his or her career ASPIRATIONS: Does the corresponding CAREER PROFILE on page 40 help to confirm the development picture?	

4. What actions need to be taken to help overcome his or her LIMITATIONS?
 	
    by him/herself:
 	
    by coaching from you:
 	
    by help from someone else (incl. off-the-job training):
 	
    specific work experience:	

5. What action needs to be taken to help the person develop his or her STRENGTHS AND POTENTIAL?
 	
    internal project/experience:
 	
    external assignment:
 	
    lateral move/ promotion:	

6. Prepare a draft DEVELOPMENT PLAN which takes note of the help above, and which you can discuss with the person when you meet at the agreed date:	

Developing Performance
links to other skills in
the Manager's Toolkit series

Each skill in this book not only links directly with other 'people' skills in the book (12), but also with other skills from the toolkit on page 13 (1, 3, 6, 8 and 10).

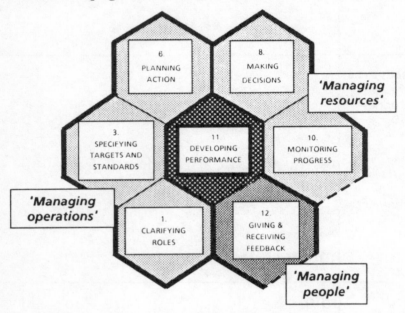

Developing performance requires an understanding of the 'operational' responsibilities of those involved in terms of roles (1) and targets (3), as well as the action planning skills (6) required to produce specific development plans.

Decisions have to be made (8) relating to development options, the selection of people and of supporting resources. The performance of those involved has to be continuously monitored (10), as does the effectiveness of the development plans themselves.

Chapter Four

GIVING AND RECEIVING FEEDBACK

GIVING AND RECEIVING FEEDBACK

Giving and receiving feedback enables you to make the most of a personal face-to-face discussion for review and development.

1. Being prepared

Talking face-to-face with individuals about how they are getting on is a critical skill but one which is particularly difficult to carry out. It is a judgemental process – 'playing God', as it has been called – and can so easily become awkward and confrontational. While we may rationally accept that everyone can benefit from personal feedback, it is an activity that can always wait until tomorrow!

First of all you need to make sure you have specific *information* about how the person has actually been performing. Without it you will be arguing about what has happened in the past instead of moving on to what needs to happen in the future. If you do not have the necessary information you should get hold of it as objectively as possible.

If there is a specific problem which needs to be addressed, determine the precise nature of the problem, ie the *evidence* of what the person concerned has actually done 'wrong', (see 'Monitoring Progress' in Volume 4, *Managing Resources*). Do you have all the relevant facts? It is too easy for prejudice,

1. Being prepared

Do you have a problem with another person which you would like to resolve?

1.1   Write down the problem with the person as you see it. Try to define what the person is actually doing wrong.

> *Jim has upset Margaret by changing the monthly reporting procedure without consulting her*

1.2   Have you the evidence to support your concern? Write it down as factually as you can.

> *Confirmed by earlier meeting with Margaret*

Do you need any additional information? How might you get it?

> *I could ask Jane. I must check with Jim*

assumption and emotion – a negative self-fulfilling prophecy – to make matters worse, particularly if the issue is a long - standing one.

Frequently people's *style* throws light on why they behave as they do. It is worth giving some thought to the relevance of 'Analyse', 'Bond' and 'Command' to the issue – both their style and yours. And how much do you know of their past experience or their domestic situation? Often a problem between people develops because they know each other only as operators in a current job and not as all-round human beings.

One of the key difficulties in 'people' problems is that those involved avoid talking it over. Because of the difficulties of doing it, the personal contact that is needed to sort things out does not take place. The issue festers, false perceptions grow and what could probably have been quickly nipped in the bud becomes a major crisis. *Courage* to be willing to talk it over is a prerequisite to any form of appraisal or counselling.

When you have accepted the fact that personal contact is essential, careful consideration needs to be given to the purpose of the meeting. What do you want to achieve by talking face-to-face? Presumably you want the problem between you to be resolved or for a particular performance improvement to take place. But how do you intend to get to that position? It needs forethought and planning.

The process of discussion will be made much easier if you carefully choose an appropriate time and place to meet. It should be a time convenient to both of you when neither of you is distracted. Similarly the location should be chosen to avoid interruptions and where both of you can feel reasonably relaxed.

1.3   *How well do you know the person?   What sort of person is he or she?*

> *Young, enthusiastic and intelligent. Doesn't see need to consult anyone!*

Does his/her personal style throw any light on the situation you have described or how you might handle it?

> *I need to encourage patience but without switching him off*

1.4   *What action are you prepared to take? Are you ready to talk face-to-face?*

> *Only face-to-face discussion will clarify the situation and help him to develop*

If you are, what result do you want from the meeting?

> *Improve Jim's relationship with Margaret.   He will see benefits of consulting and do it in future*

1.5   *Consider suitable times and places for you both to meet and select the most appropriate :*

> *Wed 9.30 am, my office - he'll be awake and is well used to discussion in my office*

2. Questioning and listening

You will not get off to a satisfactory start if you do not take great care in creating an initially relaxed atmosphere. Try to give the impression of being relaxed yourself; a smile of welcome can help, even if what you are going to talk about is no smiling matter! A cup of tea or coffee can help you both to relax. But avoid light-hearted banter or jokes in an effort to relieve the pressure; they will fall flat.

Try to keep the opening exchanges limited to sharing information which is not threatening. In view of your purpose for the meeting, what is the *key* information you need to get across early on? People rarely listen well initially in such situations, so great efforts have to be made to make sure both parties actually take in what is being said at the start when both are inevitably distracted.

If you are genuinely trying to make progress, it will be important for you to listen to and try to understand what the other person has to say. They are more likely to accept *your* point of view if they feel you have tried to understand theirs.

> **CHECKING**
> ask a question about what has just been said to ensure understanding of its content or implic-ation, eg 'Are you saying...?'

Checking understanding is therefore essential. They may even come up with information or ideas that you haven't thought of, or a dimension to the issue that has never occurred to you.

This is when it helps to deploy certain simple techniques for helping the other person to 'open up'. For example, try 'open' questions, questions that prevent a simple 'yes' or 'no' answer, such as 'How do you think...?' Allow time for shared thoughts to be digested with frequent pauses – not

2. Questioning and listening

How you are going to make sure you get the information you need?

2.1 How could you quickly establish a relaxed and positive atmosphere when you meet?	*Ask him informally about progress of recent and successful task*
2.2 In view of 1.4, what is the key information you need to get across early, and how do you propose to do it?	*Link between Margaret's performance and Jim's action*
2.3 How is the other person likely to respond? How are you going to deal with that response?	*Surprise! He'll blame M. 'She's against change; she's rude on phone.' I'll listen...*
2.4 What do you particularly need to know, and what questions should help you to get the information?	*Was this an isolated incident? How does he get on with others? Had he considered asking Margaret for her views at any point?*

all silences need to be filled. Try to add supportive grunts and 'oh yes' or 'I see' to encourage the flow of information, particularly if feelings are being revealed or personal concerns are being expressed.

It will help if you know what information you need to find out and the questions you might need to ask. Always check what the other person has just said to make sure there has been no misunderstanding. This is particularly important when you come to agree to take action to resolve the problem.

3. Planning action

Of course none of this sharing of information will be of any use if you do not move the discussion on towards action to improve the situation or to develop the person. But to do this you have to *believe* that improvement and development are actually probable – your commitment to progress has to be apparent to the other person (see page 26).

Open out your thinking about how improvement might be brought about. Try to think of the factors that are actually helping the person to improve, and all the things which are making the problem worse. Then consider how you could develop the 'helps' and overcome or diminish the 'hinders'.

Could you get someone to take him through the procedure which he doesn't understand? Can you find a way to help her get over the stressful domestic situation which is affecting her performance at the moment? (See 'Focusing on the Key Issues' in Volume 3, *Managing Information*.)

2.5   How are you going to get
       him or her to open up?
       Consider the use of these
       skills and how you might
       apply them in this
       particular situation:

       'open' questioning ☐

       allowing pauses
       and time to think ☐

       supportive 'grunts' ☐

       checking understanding ☐

                                                                    He'll have
                                  plenty to say; I'll need to check and not react at start

3. Planning action

*Do you know how to make sure that the discussion brings about
the improvement and development you want?*

3.1   What are your expect-
       ations of the outcome?
       How will it be obvious that
       you want the discussion to
       succeed?

                                  Will show my clear commitment to his development

3.2   Write down factors that are   Write down factors that are
       helping to improve the   hindering improvement:
       situation:

       Jim's keen to develop, I want to resolve...   *M's suspicious, little contact, punctual reports...*

If you have created an open and constructive atmosphere, an atmosphere in which you become a mentor or *coach* rather than an inquisitor, you are very likely to receive feedback on your *own* performance. This feedback may at first seem out of place, but can be extremely helpful to you if taken in the right spirit and viewed constructively.

If feedback and an open discussion is helpful to the other person it is probably also helpful to you. Accepting the need for you to do something new or different is also a very good way to demonstrate your personal commitment to creating a *positive* coaching environment.

You could find yourselves coming up with suggestions to overcome the weaknesses you *both* have and developing your strengths! These actions can be most effectively worked on *together*, using checking and building behaviour.

STRENGTHS   WEAKNESSES

One significant benefit to come from such a discussion will be a jointly developed and agreed *action plan*. It is important to *summarize periodically* what you have both agreed and to take informal notes. Note-taking, if done informally, demonstrates your commitment to improvement and progress. *Both of you* can then take responsibility for monitoring the results that are certain to follow.

To add to your own personal feedback, you may care to ask someone who knows you well to complete a *style questionnaire* on you, and so give you specific feedback to add to the style profile you completed for yourself on page 37. A suitable format for you to use for yourself or your team members follows, after the questionnaire, on pages 90–2.

3.3 How could you develop the 'help' factors?	How could you reduce the impact of the 'hinder' factors?
Jim to help M appreciate computer benefits with regular sessions. I'll coach him in 'people' skills as part of his personal development.	*Jim, M and I will meet to reassure M and explain importance of accurate and punctual reports. We'll discuss future changes...*

3.4 How could you encourage the other person to contribute ideas for improvement?	*Ask him for additional factors, share the list and ask him for suggestions on particular points*

3.5 Are there likely to be any actions by you which he or she may request? How will you react?	*I encouraged criticisms of M when report was late. Agree! Review situation - pressure at the time...*

3.6 How will you make sure that both of you are clear and confirm the action you have agreed? Will you need to put together an improvement/ development plan which you can then both monitor?	*Check and summarize agreed actions; both to review in 2 wks*

FEEDBACK QUESTIONNAIRE

Think back to the last time you gave someone feedback face-to-face, and consider how effective you were:

Interpersonal Skills:

How effective do think you were in using these inter-personal skills?:	DATE OF SESSION AND WITH WHOM:	*23 June 1994* *Jim Cunningham*	
Score: 'H' (too much use)	QUESTIONING	M	
'M' (about right)	CHECKING	M	RESPONDING L
'L' (too little use)	SUMMARIZING L	BUILDING M	

Giving and Receiving Feedback:

1.	What was the problem with this person that you were trying to put right?	*Jim is inclined to go ahead with his own ideas without consulting others involved, eg Margaret switched off by his changes to the monthly reporting procedure.*
2.	Were the time, place and opening conducive to establishing a relaxed and positive atmosphere?	*It was an appropriate time and he seemed to be reasonably relaxed in my office, but I should have asked Jane to take all telephone calls. I didn't need to open with another task – he knew what it was all about and we could've gone straight in.*
3.	How well did you get the initial information across and then handle the response you got?	*He understood that Margaret had switched off but didn't link it to the procedure changes. Was genuinely surprised and quick to remind me of her telephone rudeness. It was difficult not to react and not express surprise at his lack of perception.*

4.	How successful were you at getting the person to open up and provide you with the information you needed?	*The problem was justifying his behaviour initially. But after quietly letting him get it off his chest, I was able to encourage him to look at the wider issue of his relations with others.* *He eventually accepted that he was impatient with people who were not as bright as him, and who didn't see the need for change as clearly. He admitted he wasn't sure how to handle opposition to his ideas...*
5.	How far were your expectations of the outcome apparent to the other person?	*I think he felt I was getting at him at the beginning. But once he saw my concern for the development implications of his performance, and that I was willing to help him as part of his development, all was well.*
6.	How did you react to any personal feedback you received in the course of the discussion?	*I was expecting him to comment on my agreeing with him about Margaret at the time, so it was easier to handle his comments. I could easily have reacted, but instead it led to a useful discussion about the difficulty of achieving balanced judgement when under pressure.*
7.	How successful were you at getting the other person to contribute ideas to the action plan?	*He offered to help Margaret understand the benefits of computers. He was very willing to offer ideas once he stopped being defensive and realized I actually wanted his suggestions. We built on a number of each other's ideas.*

FEEDBACK QUESTIONNAIRE

Think back to the last time you gave someone feedback face-to-face, and consider how effective you were:

Interpersonal Skills:

How effective do think you were in using these inter-personal skills?:
 	
Score: 'H' (too much use)
          'M' (about right)
          'L' (too little use)
	DATE OF SESSION
	AND WITH WHOM:

DATE OF SESSION
AND WITH WHOM:

QUESTIONING	☐		
CHECKING	☐	RESPONDING	☐
SUMMARIZING	☐	BUILDING	

Giving and Receiving Feedback:

1.	What was the problem with this person that you were trying to put right?	
2.	Were the time, place and opening conducive to establishing a relaxed and positive atmosphere?	
3.	How well did you get the initial information across and then handle the response you got?	

4. How successful were you at getting the person to open up and provide you with the information you needed?	
5. How far were your expectations of the outcome apparent to the other person?	
6. How did you react to any personal feedback you received in the course of the discussion?	
7. How successful were you at getting the other person to contribute ideas to the action plan?	

Style Questionnaire

1. Score the extent to which the following statements apply to the person NOW on a scale 1–5 (1 = Not him/her; 3 = Yes, but...; 5 = Fully him/her). Circle the number (1 2 3 4 5) which is most appropriate. Then circle the number in the next column to indicate the extent to which you would like them to change this rating:

	'NOW'	'CHANGE'
1. Thinks carefully about what needs doing and why.	1 2 3 4 5	+2 +1 0 -1 -2
2. Can be relied upon to get things into perspective.	1 2 3 4 5	+2 +1 0 -1 -2
3. Is concerned that things should be done correctly.	1 2 3 4 5	+2 +1 0 -1 -2
4. Works effectively in groups.	1 2 3 4 5	+2 +1 0 -1 -2
5. Responds positively to other people's ideas.	1 2 3 4 5	+2 +1 0 -1 -2
6. Gets people organized for action.	1 2 3 4 5	+2 +1 0 -1 -2
7. Consistently keeps people informed.	1 2 3 4 5	+2 +1 0 -1 -2
8. Has no difficulty making up his/her mind.	1 2 3 4 5	+2 +1 0 -1 -2
9. Always seems to be able to get others to do what he/she wants.	1 2 3 4 5	+2 +1 0 -1 -2
10. Makes sure he/she knows how things are progressing.	1 2 3 4 5	+2 +1 0 -1 -2
11. Makes the most of what is available.	1 2 3 4 5	+2 +1 0 -1 -2
12. Prefers to deal with people face-to-face.	1 2 3 4 5	+2 +1 0 -1 -2

Reproduced with permission from *Managing People* by Peter Grainger

2. *Transfer your 'Now' scores and the 'Change' scores from the questionnaire according to the number of each statement. Add up the total 'Now' scores and highlight the most significant 'Change' scores, keeping the two sets separate:*

	'NOW' SCORES	'CHANGE' SCORES
'Analyse'		
1. Thinks carefully about what needs doing and why.	[ ]	[ ]
3. Concerned that things should be done correctly.	[ ]	[ ]
10. Makes sure he/she knows how things are progressing.	[ ]	[ ]
2. Can be relied upon to get things into perspective.	[ ]	[ ]
TOTAL	[ ]	
'Bond'		
7. Consistently keeps people informed.	[ ]	[ ]
12. Prefers to deal with people face-to-face.	[ ]	[ ]
5. Responds positively to other people's ideas.	[ ]	[ ]
4. Works effectively in groups.	[ ]	[ ]
TOTAL	[ ]	
'Command'		
9. Always seems to be able to get others to do what he or she wants.	[ ]	[ ]
6. Gets people organized for action.	[ ]	[ ]
8. Has no difficulty making up his/her mind.	[ ]	[ ]
11. Makes the most of what is available.	[ ]	[ ]
TOTAL	[ ]	

Reproduced with permission from *Managing People* by Peter Grainger

Style Profile

3. Transfer the total 'Now' scores for each 'style' from Section 2 on page 91:

'Analyse':   'Bond':   'Command':

Circle or cross the appropriate number on the model below, and then join up the points to produce the style profile. Circle those skills with the highest 'Change' scores.

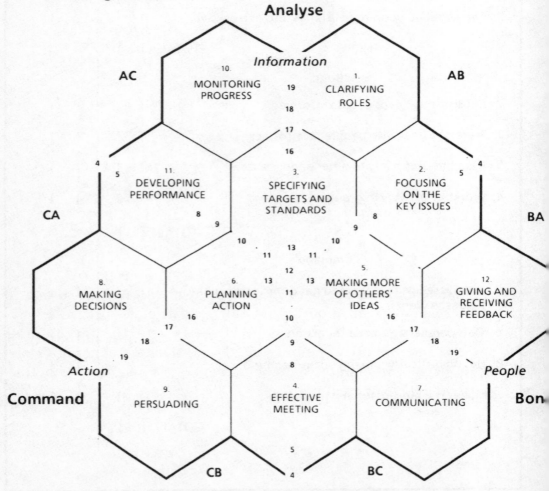

Reproduced with permission from *Managing People* by Peter Grainger

Giving and Receiving Feedback
links to other skills in
the Manager's Toolkit series

Each skill in this book not only links directly with other 'people' skills in the book (5 and 11), but also with other skills from the toolkit on page 13 (1, 3, 9 and 10).

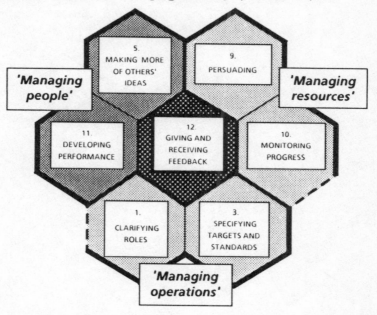

When discussing performance it is critical that the feedback results from monitoring the individual's progress (10) relating to the whole job (1) and to specific targets and standards (3). The individual may need persuading (9) on key points of improvement, as well as sharing ideas on action and development required.

Index

bold type denote main references